$\mathfrak{S}$trange
DORSET STORIES

BOSSINEY BOOKS

ACKNOWLEDGEMENTS

Front cover photography: RAY BISHOP
Back cover photography: ROB SCOTT
Other photographs: CHARLES LESLIE STUDIOS; HENDON AND
FINCHLEY TIMES; THERESA MURPHY; ROB SCOTT;
TUTANKHAMUN EXHIBITION.
Drawings: FELICITY YOUNG

First published in 1991 by
Bossiney Books, St Teath, Bodmin, Cornwall.

Typeset and printed by
Penwell Print Ltd, Callington, Cornwall.

ISBN 0 948158 69 7

Superstitions abound …

Introducing ...

DAVID FOOT, *who lives in Bristol, writes regularly on cricket, football and rugby for various newspapers, including* The Guardian *and the* Mail on Sunday. *His father was born in Dorset, and David, as a young journalist, came to know the northern part of the county.*

He has worked in radio and television and is the author of several books. His latest is Country Reporter, *an autobiographical look at local journalism and village life just after the war. His other volumes include histories of Lords' Taverners and Somerset County Cricket Club. His* Harold Gimblett, Tormented Genius of Cricket *is rated one of the finest books of its kind.* 'There has never been a cricket book quite like this,' *wrote John Arlott.* 'David Foot has written it with compassion, something not far from passion and sympathy. It is a remarkable achievement.'

More recently he has written Cricket's Unholy Trinity, *in depth studies of Charlie Parker, Jack MacBryan and Cecil Parkin, and* Sunshine, Sixes and Cider, *a history of Somerset cricket. In 1989 he introduced* Wiltshire Mysteries *and now he sets the scene for* Strange Dorset Stories.

STRANGE DORSET STORIES

David Foot

ONE particularly gruesome story, which I first heard as a small child, has remained chillingly with me. Successive generations from my home village of East Coker, just a mile or so from the Dorset border, took a spooky delight in relating every gory detail.

The incident supposedly happened deep within Penn Wood during the reign of George III. A woodman from Pendomer, the mellow hamlet beyond the parkland and hillside from Coker, was clearing the bracken to make a track when he stumbled on a smugglers' hiding place. He threw down his sickle and went on his knees to examine the chests of assorted booty. And as he did so he was clubbed to death.

By the time his mutilated body was found by another estate worker, the smugglers' haul had been moved – probably to the adjacent Coker Wood or Spin Wood. But the murder was authentic enough. When I was a young newspaper reporter I talked to an old and wise local farmer, who in his spare time had made a study of Somerset and Dorset legends. 'My father knew the dead man's family. The woodman was buried in the Pendomer churchyard.'

The Dorset coast, especially the stretch of Chesil Beach to Burton Bradstock and Lyme Regis, was notorious for smuggling. This illicit trafficking was big and profitable business. Much went undetected. There was a ready market for the brandy and wines, silks and lace. Some went, by devious routes to the big houses: lawlessness of this sort knew no obvious social demarcation lines. Nor did a little bribery. Those whose duty it was to keep law and order were occasionally encouraged to turn a blind eye.

But great and often brave efforts were made to curb the smugglers. The death of the Pendomer woodman was far from an isolated fatality. For the transporting of the booty, brought mostly from

7

France and the Channel Islands, was a thoroughly hazardous business. 'Them French do know every little creak and cranny in the Dorset coast', it used to be said. Yet the landing of the illegal consignments was for the network of smugglers only half the battle.

Then began the transfer, via the tortuous Dorset lanes, to the shady merchants and, in some cases, to mansions in West Somerset. There had to be well-obscured 'storehouses' en route. The woods at Penn and Coker, in a fairly direct line through Bridport and Beaminster towards Exmoor and the Quantocks, were a convenient smugglers' depot.

Fiction has given the whole nefarious trade a romantic gloss. But in truth it was often brutal. There was too much at risk for it to be anything else. The smugglers and their hand-picked recruits, found in the coastal taverns of Swanage, Weymouth or Lyme, travelled by night. They used pack horses. They knew the short cuts, the unpopulated by-ways. At times, at the dead of night, simple village people would hear the eerie clatter of hooves. It made them tremble.

In the morning, they would ask one another: 'Did 'e hure them hosses in the night. Were 'um ghosts?'

'More likely them smugglers up vrom Bridport . . . '

Strange noises . . . strange happenings . . . at a strange hour. Just one of many strands in the strange stories of Dorset.

In 1984 Bossiney publisher Michael Williams invited me, to my eternal surprise, to introduce *Strange Somerset Stories*. He apparently decided it made sense to ask 'a cynical professional journalist' to set the scene. He accepted that as an incorrigible sceptic I might take some convincing. Maybe one can become too objective; all I can say is that in putting my instant thoughts on to paper, I have been enthralled by my research. Some of the stories have made me chuckle. Some have made me snort and reject. Rather a lot have made me uneasy.

Michael himself is a persuasive man. He has to be if his bible is Wisden and his favourite team Gloucestershire. I have yet to discover how a Cornishman came to be riveted by the deeds of Grace, Hammond, Procter and Jack Russell. Strange that, Mr Williams: maybe the genesis of another of your books of enigma, sometime.

He is, I know, a member of the Ghost Club and has been investigating the supernatural for more than a quarter of a century. The

… via the tortuous Dorset lanes …

other day he told me: 'I'm not surprised to find so much supernatural material in Dorset. There is a tremendous atmosphere in parts of the county – and so much has taken place inside these boundaries. Here in some places I get the feeling that the thing we call TIME is like a film. It may become tangled or twisted and, as a result, we pick up fragments of *other* times.'

Michael Williams is absolutely right when he says, in effect, that Dorset has a paradoxical appeal. It's patently so beautiful and English – and yet has much violence lurking beneath the surface. Any criminologist will cite the county as the location for more than its share of grisly murders. Theories about the identification of Jack the Ripper far outnumber his victims, documented or otherwise, though one school of research into the macabre maintains he was a Dorset man. Terence Rattigan's famous play *Cause Célèbre* had strong links with Bournemouth, embraced these days by Dorset.

As a junior reporter, working for a weekly newspaper just after the war, I had at times to cycle around the country lanes of north

...patently so beautiful and English ...

10

Dorset. I fell in love with the charming names of villages like Melbury Osmond and Ryme Intrinsica. I always paused at the latter to look at the remains of a cottage where once, according to my elders, a witch lived and offered unconventional aids to health and well-being.

There was always much talk of the shameful past: of the Bloody Assizes, of course, and Judge Jeffreys' unmitigated evil judgments. Of the disquieting activities of Jack Ketch, the public hangman and his assistant, who doubled-up appositely as a butcher. You'll still find 'Hangman's Cottage' on one or two gnarled old country gates.

'Terrible things happened to Monmouth's followers, you know. They put up gallows at Lyme Regis, Weymouth and Bridport'. And, I wanted to add, at Melcombe Regis, Wareham and a few other places besides. Apart from the hangings, there were the public floggings on many a Dorset village green. Dorchester itself, noble and handsome county town, groaned with ghastly deeds.

When I read Hardy first, I was puzzled over the pervasive pessimism in his prose. Yet he was a quintessential Dorset man, who must have agonised over what had gone on at Jeffreys' behest. As a child he went on long, solitary walks. He saw the deprivations suffered by the rural communities in the county. Once he came across the shrivelled body of a farm labourer in a ditch; he'd died of malnutrition.

Every county is moulded by its specific sense of history. Dorset's goes back a long, long way, even if not quite as far as neighbouring Wiltshire's. The earthworks remain for all to see and wonder about. And through the centuries that followed, there was much tragedy, many dark deeds. The famous ruins of Corfe Castle continue to stand aloft, reminding us uneasily of Edward the Martyr's murder there, probably on the instructions of his stepmother, and the starving to death of the Duke of Brittany in the dungeons.

There have always been tears. The suffering caused by the horrific fire at Blandford in 1731 could never be forgotten. Wareham and Dorchester also had their serious fires. Old Dorset men and women still point out where the ghastly blazes are said to have started, still argue about the way blame was apportioned.

With the succeeding years of intermittent misery went, inexorably, legend and rumour. Some said Brownsea Island, close to

Poole Harbour, had a strange, unfathomable background. Others found it hard to explain the warren of mainland underground tunnels, real and imagined, or the persistent tale of hidden treasures just off the road between Bere Regis and Wimborne. An ancient villager from Yetminster, with perhaps too unwieldy an imagination and clearly susceptible to blood-curdling stories passed on by previous generations of her family, once assured me: 'There's been so much unnecessary bloodshed in Dorset. I love the place but it's got an aura of evil that won't go away.'

She warmed to her theme and pointed out that the suave multi-killer Neville Heath was drawn to the chines of Bournemouth for some of his murkier activities. I tried to put the record straight by saying that Bournemouth was still part of Hampshire then. Heath was, in fact, the only monster-criminal I ever met. It was only a month or so before he was arrested and of course I had no knowledge of his intent. But his conversation was strange (to pursue the theme of the book!) and full of sexual innuendo. At this distance, it strikes me that he wouldn't have been fastidious, Dorset or Durham, over the location for his gratification.

My father was born in Dorset: in the middle of a wood at Upcerne. It must have been desperately lonely, and even eerie in the bleak depths of winter. Superstitions abounded in that corner of the county; it wasn't far from the hillside giant, famous for his manifested manhood and the fertility rituals that he was said to encourage. I once asked my father if he had been frightened, growing up with just the trees for company. 'Only by the snakes in the summer,' he joked.

Some of the things that went on within the boundary of Dorset were certainly no laughing matter. Take the case of John Calcraft, one of the county's twenty MPs (Corfe with a relatively small population had two) in 1831. He was that rarity for the times, a temperate Tory with a point of view that veered to open-mindedness. When it came to the parliamentary Reform Bill, introduced by the Whig Lord Grey, Calcraft offered his moral support.

Such moderation earned instant rebuke from his ranks. He was pilloried by his colleagues, bitterly criticised by some he thought were his friends for allegedly 'changing sides'. The taunts continued and became too much for him. He killed himself.

That should have troubled a few Dorset consciences. So should

The infamous Judge Jeffreys.

something that happened at Maumbury Rings nearly 130 years earlier.

Thousands of ghouls poured from Dorchester and the surrounding countryside for the public strangling of a pretty teenager called Mary Channing. She was just nineteen and was brutally killed by the hangman because, on highly contested evidence, she had been found guilty of poisoning her husband, a tetchy old man she had been forced to marry.

She continued to protest her innocence to the last seconds – against a conflicting cacophony of strident cries of 'Burn the young witch!' to 'Save poor Mary – it weren't her!' The hangman, paid not to reason, did his macabre duty. The reluctant bride's head sagged – and the hundreds of onlookers trudged home, troubled by what they'd seen and ashamed that they had gone along to gloat.

Dorset was not responsible for the cruel vagaries of the judiciary. Yet the county still had reasons for shame. In the blood-lusting spirit of the times, there was the impassioned bear-baiting that went on at established venues like Marnhull, and cockfighting, for big stakes and fiendish delight, all round the county. The annual competitions at Wimborne brought spectators from miles away.

When it came to politics, corruption was as rife in Dorset – maybe worse – than in other parts of the country. The elections at Shaftesbury in 1774 were an unmitigated disgrace. There were three candidates – and two places. 'Twenty guineas for two votes' was the open invitation. At the Red Lion, as it was then, there was no attempt at subterfuge. Cash was eagerly passed through a hole in the door.

Voting was often a mockery. Private arrangements between their lordships were far too common. The result could be violence at the Town Hall, as was the case in 1826 at Weymouth. The officials barricaded themselves in. But rioters eventually barged their way in, 'laying into the Mayor and scattering documents'. Politics has a lot to answer for in Dorset. When the Reform Bill was rejected in the Lord's, there were violent scenes in many parts of the county. Sherborne Castle was severely damaged by an organised gang. My grandmother, who worked in service at the castle half a century later, listened to accounts of what went on.

We cannot expect to absolve ourselves completely from the inhumanity of those who came before. In the same way, Dorset still fidgets uncomfortably when it comes, as it must, to the Tolpuddle Martyrs. All we have left are the old sycamore where the farm labourers met, and the half dozen cottages put up by the TU Congress in the mid-30s. Corporate consciences can never be salved.

Charges were trumped up. Decent men, five of them devout Methodists, were made out to be criminals. The magistrates came out of the corrupt legal scandal with dishonour claiming they were mainly making an example of the defendants. The Church had no reason at all to be proud of itself. The men's employers connived with the local establishment to ensure that their interpretation of justice was a fait-accompli. Deportation was a horrid penalty.

There were many strange aspects to the case. Names like Loveless Standfield, Hammett and Brine were ennobled for ever. But why, after they had returned to Dorset, did several of them decide to emigrate to Canada? They always refused to say publicly. Were they choosing to reject the land they had tilled but which, perhaps they felt, had betrayed them?

Others in this book will no doubt write of the ghosts. I have heard or read of, shall we say, a tenth of them: of the phantom coaches at Lulworth and Beaminster, the headless coachman at Loders, the haunted bridge at Holnest where the coach and horses plunged into a deep stream and vanished for ever. There's a persistent tale about coffins appearing in the middle of the road at Gillingham and Wimborne – and then, just as suddenly, disappearing again. Again on a personal level – for which I hope I'll be forgiven – I had a relative in north Dorset who had strange gifts and powers with domestic pets and fowls (I used to watch him hypnotise hens in the most uncanny way).

'How do you do it?', I asked, as a rapt schoolboy.

'We're strange people in rural Dorset', he used to say. I feel I must add one more sad strand to the memory. My relative, sound of mind and body, mysteriously hanged himself a few years later.

It isn't all melancholy, of course – far from it. Dorset is a county of exquisite charm. Not simply the glamorized and glorious Milton Abbas and Shaftesbury's Gold Hill; but the pastoral stretches of the Blackmore Vale, the towns and villages built alongside the Stour, Frome and Puddle, the thatched cottages, the swans at Abbotsbury, the smallest pub, the dozens of remote streams . . . .

… coffins appearing in the middle of the road …

Not just the historic grandeur of Dorchester itself and the hon-eyed loveliness of Sherborne, which enchanted Raleigh; but the chalk hills, Hardy's awesome healthlands, the handsome, distinc-tive coastline ever dredging up its sheer mysteries from the time-less seas, the stillness and lack of motorways, the all-powerful silence of history.

King Alfred was seduced by it. So was William Barnes, who told his dialect tales with sweet poetic gentleness. And so was Lawrence of Arabia who needed to be neither Ross nor Shaw with-in the anonymity of Cloud's Hill. Lawrence, most complex of men, *strangest* of mortals, found Dorset a potent, conducive atmosphere – similar to the desert itself – to sit and philosophise.

Turner and Constable came with their sketch-pads, Augustus John to stay. Henry Fielding, soon to be a great novelist, dreamed here at East Stour as a lad. Jane Austen was reluctant to leave the county, as was Wordsworth.

And what of the eccentrics who, over the generations, outnum-bered the smugglers in Dorset? Gulliver the Garrulous was surely one. He was the arch entrepreneur of coastal illegality. He wore a facade of thorough respectability as he strutted the streets of Swanage. Many secretly admired his administrative skills, merce-nary and lawless as they were. Long after his death, relatives in the Charlton Marshall area spoke with some understandable pride of his smuggling prowess.

Yet he wasn't memorably eccentric in the sense of many endear-ing and doddery lords of the manor, not in the class of that extraor-dinary squire Tregonwell Frampton, for instance.

We inevitably associate Moreton, near to Bovington, with Lawrence. But for human quirkiness, Frampton can hardly be ignored. If he had lived today, he'd have been an influential horse owner who never missed a Newmarket sale and was always in the gossip columns. He liked horses – and Newmarket, where he was buried – as much as the manor house at Moreton, where a brass portrait of his ancestors, James Frampton (1532) showed the origi-nal squire kneeling in prayer.

Tregonwell was maybe a trifle more irreligious. He was one of the great gamblers of his day.

His knowledge of horses, many of which he bred himself and sold at a handsome profit, much impressed William III – so much

The all-powerful silence of history …

so, in fact, that he appointed him trainer of the royal horses. That was what Frampton remained for more than 30 years. When he died he was grandly described as 'the keeper of the running horses of their majesties William III, Queen Anne, George I and George II.'

For someone who moved in such elevated circles, he made no concessions when it came to his wardrobe. His appearance was hardly that of a Dorset squire. His contemporaries joked that he didn't appear to have a second suit. Perhaps he needed a woman around to smarten him up. But Tregonwell was a misogynist, infinitely more in love with his horses. No wife, in any case, would ever have forgiven him in those days for losing as he occasionally did, £1,000 on a race, the fortunes of a fighting cock or the turn of a card.

Quite apart from Newmarket, Dorset liked a flutter in its own right. There were races at Blandford and records show a racecourse was set up at Tarrant Monkton. The local clergy, who often had private means to supplement the modest stipend, relished a surreptitious bet. A surreptitious drink, too, if we're to believe some of the reports of slurred words in the pulpit.

The history of the county reverberates intriguingly with the variegated whims of strange people and the breath-catching accounts of strange happenings. And the flavour is captured by the miscellany in this book.

I come finally to *The Tempest*, for a reason I'll explain in a moment. Let me quote Herbert Farjeon on it: *'It is the loveliest of all Shakespeare's plays . . . it has always seemed to me the most baffling flight of beauty that ever called for an audience of poets . . . it has the smell of the sea-shore and the sound is that of a shell against the ear, when all the storms and zephyrs that have ever swept the seas make peace in a cool, echoing whisper.'*

Prospero's Island, as Shakespeare saw it, was Bermuda to more prosaic souls like you and me. It was discovered by Sir George Somers, born at Lyme Regis and sometime, between voyages, mayor of the coastal town. Somers was a seafaring adventurer. His adventures, stranger than any fiction, inspired Shakespeare to write his last, and many would say his best, play.

Next time I see The Tempest, I'll think of Dorset.

Introducing ...

THERESA MURPHY, born in Portland, is a regular contributor of fiction and non-fiction to national and international magazines, and is a member of the high intelligence society MENSA.

Her book Murder in Dorset *was published by Robert Hale in 1988, while her first novel is due out shortly, and another true crime book is to be published nationally in the summer of 1991.*

Theresa has also contributed to television comedy programmes. In addition, she has many and varied literary projects in the pipeline.

An avid off-road driver, she is the proud owner of a huge American Jeep.

Here in her debut for Bossiney, Theresa Murphy recalls a strange sad story whose bottom line has to be left unwritten . . .

CROSS OF TRAGEDY

Theresa Murphy

A TOURIST's delight, Dorset has many places of interest. To travel from the rocky stark beauty of Portland through the golden sands and past the kiss-me-quick trippers of Weymouth on to the grandeur of Bournemouth, is easily to understand the attraction that the county holds.

Yet, away from the main traffic-packed roads, so tiny that those passing rarely see it, is a cross of tragedy, a memorial to a holiday of long ago that went terribly wrong. Embedded in the roadside bank just over the first rise on the lonely road from Bere Regis to Wareham, is a crude cross of stones. Nature has, over many passing summers and bleak winters, encroached upon the little memorial, but in more recent years a white upright cross has been added. Though this makes the spot more easily noticeable, the new cross bears just a date, 1928, as an enigmatic message to frustrate and intrigue the curious passer-by.

Though ending in Dorset with a pathos no dramatist could conjure into a work of fiction, the story begins in Catford, a South East borough of London. It was there, at 147, Laleham Road, a thoroughfare of smart, sturdy houses, that an excited 14-years-old girl packed for an August holiday in 1928. For Iris Willis, a city girl, there was magic in the anticipation of a vacation in the depths of rural Dorset, although the name of the village in which she was to stay, Piddletrenthide, caused her a delighted and secret giggle or two.

Nothing is perfect, however, and the blot on the holiday horizon to Iris was the fact that her father, Richard James Willis, to whom she was deeply attached, had to remain behind at home.

Iris's love was reciprocated, and by means of considerable but concealed self-sacrifice, Richard Willis eased his daughter's pain at

Where it all began – Laleham Road in London, the home of Iris Willis who travelled to her death on a Dorset hillside.

being parted by promising to take a day excursion to Dorset in the middle of the following week – Wednesday August 22, 1928.

Fortified by this pledge, Iris climbed happily into the Morris Cowley car driven by chiropodist David Evans, who, with his cousin Muriel Evans, and his mother, accompanied Iris on the holiday.

Those were the days when motoring belonged to the few, the privileged, and the roads were quiet as they skirted the south of London and drove down the A30, the increasingly rustic countryside drawing squeals of joy from both Iris and Muriel Evans, who was about her age.

Even so, as they put a greater distance between themselves and the London left behind, Iris's spirits sagged, for she was already missing her father – a fact Mrs Evans was quick to notice.

'Come on, now, Iris, chin up,' she encouraged the little passenger. 'Just enjoy yourself and know that your dad will be down to see you on Wednesday. He will come to a seaside town named Swanage. We can spend the day with him there. It's only twenty miles away.'

'Twenty miles', sighed Iris unhappily. 'By the time we get there we won't have much time left to be with dad.'

'Absolute nonsense, Iris,' said David Evans. 'I'll drive you down to Swanage, and I promise that I will have you at that railway station before your father's train arrives.'

At this Iris brightened up, and she was soon pointing out various things along the way to her friend.

The two girls were still shrilling their delight when the car neared Dorchester and made its way through meandering lanes.

'Nearly there, girls,' the driver told them as he took a sharp left turn to let the car roll quietly over the last few yards of the journey into the gate of Mill Farm at Piddletrenthide, where they were greeted by a smiling Mrs Brooks.

The genuine welcome of Mrs Brooks heralded the beginning of wonderful days for Iris. Accustomed to asphalt foot and roadways, crowded with people, made hazardous by vehicular traffic, she couldn't get enough of the open green fields, the flowers, and the farm animals. The days passed quickly.

They were all up bright and early the day Iris's father was expected.

With David Evans already behind the wheel of the car, Iris stood back dutifully so that Mrs Evans could get into the front passenger seat beside her son, while she, Iris, would join Mrs Brooks and Muriel in the rear seat.

'No, no, Iris,' smiled Mrs Evans. 'This is your day, and you must take pride of place in the front seat.'

So that was the seating arrangement as the Morris Cowley drove out on to the road in the direction of Dorchester, then, with Iris and Muriel singing, made a sharp left turn on the first leg of the journey to Swanage.

Skilfully guiding the car out of Bere Regis, David drove along the road to Poole a short distance before coming to the crossroads that had Woodbury Hill on the left, and the road to the poetically-named Sugar Hill on the right. Giving a clear signal, David Evans swung the car right on the way to Sugar Hill, and even Mrs Evans, herself unused to the countryside, gave a little gasp of astonishment at the sheer unspoilt beauty of the area.

'Swanage next stop,' David said to Iris as the car gamely tackled the short rise to the brow of Sugar Hill. 'On the way you'll see the ancient monument of Corfe Castle.'

It was all so wonderful, and passengers and driver alike looked forward to enjoying the panoramic view they knew was just ahead of them.

Things though, weren't so wonderful for lorry driver George Greening, who was having trouble with his lorry as he climbed Sugar Hill from the other direction, coming up the less sharp but longer gradient from Wareham. What was the problem that Greening, an ex-Tank Corps man then living at Virginia House, Langton Matravers was experiencing? It was to become a matter of life and death and the answer was never discovered.

What was never in doubt was that the lorry owned by Swanage

On an August morning in 1928 a happy Iris Willis was driven out of this junction on her way to meet her father at Swanage..

Sugar Hill as the lorry driver would have seen it on that fateful morning. The roadside cross is on the right of the picture close to the top of the hill.

haulage contractor Mr Lucas, and loaded with tarmac was on the wrong side of the road when the Morris Cowley, driven by David Evans, came over the hill.

Neither driver had a chance of avoiding a collision, and the Morris car slammed with a metal-grinding sound head-on into the lorry. The terrific impact caused the car's petrol tank, located under the bonnet, to explode, sending the whole vehicle instantly up in flames.

The explosion and rush of flames brought a young forestry worker running to the scene. He had seen the lorry zig-zagging up the hill, and though he hadn't seen the actual crash, he realised that the worst had happened.

Mrs Brooks had been thrown from the car into the road by the impact, as had David Evans, and the forestry worker helped first Mrs Brooks and then David Evans to the bank, where sat the injured Mrs Evans and Muriel.

'I thought that was it,' the forestry worker said years later. 'Though some of them were hurt, and the lorry driver was in an hysterical state, I was thinking it could have been a lot worse. Then I happened to look at where the flames had apparently set the bank alight. What I saw was horrific, made more terrible because there was nothing that could done. A little girl, covered from head to foot with burning petrol, had been thrown out of the car onto the bank. As I looked on, sick and helpless, she became nothing but a charred skeleton.'

Iris Willis, just 14 years old, had died horribly, her ghastly remains lying that morning in the exact position later to be marked by Dorset's mystery cross.

Though there weren't many cars around on that lonely road, the next one along, by incredible coincidence, was driven by a doctor who gave first aid to the injured, but could only shake a head over poor Iris Willis.

More were soon at the scene of the accident, including Police Constable Jay from Bere Regis, RAC man Harris who lived on that road, and Richard Monk, a Bere Regis motor engineer called out initially to clear the road, and then give a professional opinion as to the condition of the vehicles prior to the collision.

In a critical condition, Mrs Evans was taken to Poole General Hospital, while Mrs Brooks, severely injured, was nearer her home, in the County Hospital at Dorchester.

Someone had the unenviable task of meeting Richard Willis from the train at Swanage to tell him that his beloved daughter was dead. Not surprisingly, a week and one day later at an inquest held in Wareham, the bereaved Mr Willis was overcome by emotion.

Also badly affected, and giving his evidence with extreme difficulty, was David Evans, the driver, who one moment had a bright, cheerful girl sitting at his side, and a few seconds later saw her as a cinder of a corpse that would remain in his mind for the rest of his life. The distress of the father, and the driver who was so close to the dead girl, can be measured by the fact that policeman Jay, an outsider called to the scene in his line of duty, fainted while giving evidence and fell heavily to the floor.

Though a due process of law, there would seem to be little to gain from the inquiry – the dead girl couldn't be brought back, the discomfort of the injured could not be eased by it, and there was no way that the terrible memories seared into the minds of all those involved could be erased.

Yet there was the big question WHY? On a little-used road, how could two vehicles, with plenty of room to pass, come to collide? Anticipating that this would be the crux of the inquest, the lorry's owner had solicitor A.W. Malin keeping a watching brief at the inquiry.

One vital witness, the young forestry worker who had actually seen the lorry going from one side to the other of the road as it climbed the hill, and had assumed that the vehicle did not have the power to pull its 5-ton load directly up the hill, was not called. In retrospect that perhaps poses a bigger question than any at the inquest.

All that remained of the tragic Iris Willis was her charred bones and a few metal particles from clothes that she had been wearing that morning, and this was the only evidence, medical or otherwise that could possibly be offered.

Bravely battling against his distress, David Evans told the court of the seating arrangements in the car, and of how he'd come over the top of the hill on his correct side of the road at a speed of about 30mph.

'When I first saw the lorry it was on its own side of the road, but began to come over towards us. I noticed this right away, but assumed that the driver would correct this. He didn't. I braked at once, but I could not avoid a collision with the lorry that was by then squarely in front of my car.'

'What distance was the lorry from your car when you first saw it?' David Evans was asked.

'25 to 50 yards away,' replied Evans, who had been set afire and injured in the crash, although allowed to leave hospital after treatment.

Though doubtlessly given sincerely, this answer has to be inaccurate when it is borne in mind that the stone cross, situated close to the top of the hill, marks the exact spot where Iris burned to death, and the fact that the heavily-laden lorry was moving at less than a crawling speed.

That the steering of the lorry had been unsuspectedly defective, was a theory put forward, supported at first, by the Bere Regis motor engineer asked by the police to examine the vehicle.

This answer was reassuring for the owner of the lorry, but the astute coroner wouldn't leave it at that, and he put a question to Richard Monk that must have been in the minds of quite a few present.

'You have said that this part was fractured. What would be needed to have it break away completely?'

A good question. If the lorry had been on the wrong side of the road for some other reason – like being unable to pull its load straight up the hill, then the impact with the car may have snapped the steering arm.

'A blow could have caused it to break away finally,' answered Monk, causing the solicitor to get to his feet again.

'Could the arm have snapped away without any outside influence whatsoever?'

'Yes,' said Monk, to the relief of the solicitor and his client.

Then it was the turn of the lorry driver to give evidence: 'I was climbing the hill at about 4mph. The lorry started to cross to the other side of the road, and I found that I couldn't get it back. There was no way for a collision to be avoided, and the car hit my lorry and burst into flames.'

All in the courtroom seemed content with this answer. A little girl died horrifically because of a broken lorry component that caused the heavy vehicle to cross involuntarily to the other side of the road. But the foreman of the jury spotted a loophole.

'If you were going up a hill so slowly, and you found that your steering was not answering to your steering wheel,' said the juryman. 'Surely it would have been a simple matter in those circumstances to declutch, apply your brakes and bring the lorry to a halt?'

'Not necessarily,' was driver Greening's totally inadequate answer, but the question was dropped at that stage.

'That lorry didn't just go across the road once,' said the forestry worker who had witnessed it at the time. 'It was going from one side to the other from the time I first saw it until I heard the crash.'

Had he been in court making that statement on oath, then the outcome of the inquest could have been different.

With no independent eye witness in court, the coroner exonerated the lorry driver from blame, and the jury returned a verdict of accidental death.

The verdict is history. Yet the memory of Iris Willis has lived on down the long years, through the multiple tragedies of world war, and it is not possible to visit her lowly roadside shrine without finding it cared for with at least one flower placed there in remembrance.

Who has cared, and still continues to care, for that memorial is one of the mysteries of Dorset that is likely to forever remain unsolved. The road worker who lived in Bere Regis was once the

The destination a young girl never reached – Swanage station where Iris was to meet her father.

unofficial caretaker – but he has long since retired and gone to his own grave. Another theory is that gypsies tend it, which is given some credence by the fact that Romanies do mark a tragic spot so, but only for fellow gypsies.

Others think that the only one in the car unhurt, Muriel Evans, has taken care of the cross in loving memory of her young friend. This may well be so, but Muriel would be elderly now, and frequent journeys to Sugar Hill, which is barren in winter and prone to all the hazards of today's fast and heavy motor traffic, would be a strain.

Has the upkeep of the memorial been the work of just one person, or of a secret continuum?

Someone, somewhere, knows the answer, but to share that answer would largely destroy the living legend of Sugar Hill.

Though the bottom line has to be left unwritten, at least those countless visitors to Dorset who, every year, come upon the mystery cross and write to the national newspapers for an explanation, now know the tragic story of a little girl who, like them, came to Dorset for a holiday, but found an early and a terrible death instead.

Introducing ...

DAVID YOUNG, with his dogs William and Oliver, is a familiar figure on Television South West screens, and through his television work he has made many visits to Dorset.

David Foot says 'As befits an architect – a perceptive and outspoken one – he introduces us to some of the county's weird and wonderful buildings. It will be indirectly an old boys' reunion; we haven't met for a long time but went to the same school together, just down evocative Babylon Hill from Dorset.'

David Young's earlier books for Bossiney were Around Glorious Devon *and* Somerset in the Old Days.

WEIRD AND WONDERFUL BUILDINGS

David Young

DORSET has its fair share of strange and unusual buildings, some of which rank among the finest in the country and they are not all 'Follies' by any means. Take the Umbrella House at **Lyme Regis** for example, a delightful little building. Originally a toll house it was later owned by an architect who made two strangely attractive alterations. He added a carved sixteenth century Flemish front door and placed carved owls as capitals to the supporting columns. The entire building is capped by its 'umbrella' roof of thatch, a roof shape ideal for shedding rain. Native huts, for instance, are always circular with a cone or umbrella shaped roof. This charming little house was built a long time before umbrellas were ever used in this country but, who knows, perhaps it was the inspiration for their design?

In the 1870s and 1880s George Burt was creating, in **Swanage**, something that might well have been the inspiration behind Sir Clough Williams-Ellis's Welsh fantasy village Portmeirion – the famous location for the weird TV series 'The Prisoner' – using his uncle John Mowlem's building firm, still a major contractor today, he salvaged major bits and pieces from the City of London, as it was demolished and re-installed some of the 'best bits' in the town.

Swanage is much enhanced by his so called 'follies'. From London Bridge came the superb blank-faced clock tower, two massive Ionic columns that stand in the Grosvenor Hotel car park, an archway from Hyde Park Corner, a couple of headless statues of Charles I and a Chinese pavilion complete with dragon and iron columns from Billingsgate were all brought west.

Burt's Durlston Castle was built as a restaurant and all along the side of the castle are educational inscriptions of geographical and astronomical detail.

Most famous of all is the Great Globe. With a diameter of 10 feet

Built a long time before the introduction of umbrellas to England - but was this charming little cottage perhaps the inspiration for their design?

it weighs 40 tons and is surrounded by plaques with inscriptions on every available place including a plea to possible rival graffiti artists to use only one particular stone for their autographs, a wish faithfully observed. As we are prone to say of such folk today 'Shall we see his like again?'. I doubt it, most of London's contemporary buildings are built of fragile fabrics and are unlikely to stand long enough to enjoy the chance of a move to the seaside.

A fragile fabric that was successfully restored can be seen in the only church in the world where all the windows are entirely of engraved glass – St. Nicholas Church in **Moreton**. The church was bombed by German raiders in 1940 destroying all the original stained glass. With the help of war damage money the church was gradually rebuilt with the delightful and unique addition of magnificent engraved glass windows by Laurence Whistler. Later windows were paid for privately as memorials. One window traces the bombing and rebuilding of the church whilst the central window in the apse contains emblems of the Passion. Lovliest of all is the family memorial window depicting the seasons. Each one is contained within a bubble encircling a central sun. These unique and beautifully engraved windows must surely rank amongst Dorset's finest treasures.

In complete contrast to the elegant but simple engraved windows in Moreton church is a highly ornate marble memorial to James Frampton's wife Mary, who died in 1760 at the age of 36. Her husband's tribute is written in verbose, flowery language and with a charmingly sincere list of sentiments.

'She was a rare example of true conjugal affection and of those amiable qualities on which alone are founded the charms of domestic happiness. The advantages she enjoyed of a very ample fortune, an engaging manner and a pleasing form were far surpassed by the inestimable endowments of her mind, by her modesty and gentleness of manner, cheerfulness and sweetness of temper, good sense and unaffected piety with a most exemplary patience and resignation under the severe trials of a lingering, painful illness. These virtues endeared her to all ranks of people and rendered her, during the union of sixteen years, the comfort and delight of her husband, who truly sensible of her uncommon merit and his own unhappiness in the loss of so excellent a person whom he most highly esteemed and dearly loved, erected this monument as a testimony of his affection, grief and gratitude.'

What a charming couple they must have been.

A memorial to someone more publicly known was rejected by a cathedral but found its home in a simple Dorset church. A splendid effigy of Lawrence of Arabia was originally designed for the south aisle of Salisbury Cathedral but had to be rehoused elsewhere because the Dean refused to accept it. You will find it however in the tiny Saxon church of St. Martin at **Wareham**. The enormous tomb, its size out of proportion to the simple little church, dwarfs its surroundings. It depicts a reclining effigy of Lawrence dressed in full Arabic costume. The carving by Eric Kennington is superb and the Rector of Wareham wisely decided, because of Lawrence's many local Dorset connections, that the effigy should be allowed pride of place in this charming little church.

A staunch friendship is commemorated by an imposing monument standing proudly on the ridge of Blackdown Hill near **Portesham**. Hardy's Monument is built to immortalise Lord Nelson's Flag Captain, Admiral Sir Thomas Masterman Hardy, famous for receiving Lord Nelson's final death bed words: 'Kiss Me Hardy', though some believe Nelson said 'Kismet, Hardy' – meaning fate. An ugly chimney-like tower, erected by public subscription in 1844, it survives today and is well worth the climb if only to enjoy the fabulous views. One of the National Trust's earliest properties, it was acquired by them back in 1900.

Follies come in all shapes and sizes – resplendent on the top of **Creech Hill** is one of the earliest eye-catching follies in the country, dating from 1746 and owned by Denis Bond of the family which gave London's Bond Street its name. The stone archway is a pure folly built only to provide a romantic vista from the house. It is really best seen from the back where it can be viewed permanently in silhouette from the house below. Made of grey, now lichen-covered, stone, this simple and elegant arch was given to the National Trust in 1942.

But surely one of the finest folly towers in Britain was built by Edward Drax, the then owner of **Charlborough**, in 1790. Standing in one of Dorset's more splendid parks, the tower was struck by lightning in 1838, was damaged, and rebuilt in 1839 by John Erle Drax. He built it forty feet higher, making a total height of 100 feet. A fine Gothic tower, it has five storeys with buttresses riding two storeys, lancet windows and balustraded battlements. The approach to this folly is magnificent, a long grassy avenue flanked by mono-

Originally designed for a cathedral this splendid effigy of Lawrence of Arabia now rests in a humble country church.

lithic plinths, a balustraded bridge and a flight of steps to the tower. Inside is a superb staircase, stone-built with iron balustrades, both attractive and functional which is unusual in a folly and there is a grotesque bearded head on the banister rail. The prospect room at the top allows incredible views over five counties. The Draxs have left to posterity a fine folly which for once was built to last.

Another 'room with a view' is the **Clavel Tower** which stands sad, desolate and dilapidated, battered by winter's storms, on an exposed site on the headland above Kimmeridge Bay. It was built in 1820 by Rev John Richards – who later took the name Clavell when he inherited the Smedmore estate – in order to enjoy his views in comfort. They are indeed superb views over the bay and cliffs. The tower is circular and the lower part is surrounded by a colonnade for which the basement forms a projecting podium. There was even a fireplace on every floor. The tower was built from stucco covered stone with brick surrounds on the doors and windows. Its owner spent 13 years enjoying his own folly before his death in 1833. Because of its air of desolation and unusual position it has proved popular with film makers over the years.

A watch tower with a difference stands on the county boundary between Dorset and Wiltshire. **Horton Tower** is known as 'Sturt's folly'. It is really a prospect tower built on high ground during the 1760s as an observatory, enabling its owner Humphrey Sturt to observe the deer in his surrounding estate. Although a massive and certainly ugly building of red brick it is a brilliant architectural exercise for it converts from a triangle in the lower storeys to a hexagon higher up. The transition is skilfully concealed by three circular turrets with ball and dome tops. It is even more unusual inside for in spite of the lack of roof and floors it is pure hexagon from top to bottom. A most complicated and intricate structure for so simple a need as spotting a few deer.

From sublime views to the more mundane site of the monks' wash house in **Sherborne**. The abbey conduit, one of the oldest of the many lovely ancient buildings in the charming town of Sherborne is a little gem. It is to be found at the end of Cheap Street and was the work of Abbot Frith in about 1350. The conduit was used by the monks for their ablutions and later in its history as a market shelter. During the last century doors were fitted and for a short while it became the town's library. Thankfully it is now fully restored and shows up to great advantage against a backcloth of black and white timbered houses. It has a lovely vaulted roof and fine traceried windows and is a splendid and well preserved example of an abbey conduit.

A perfect example of a parish church built on a pagan site is at **Knowlton**. The surrounding earth circle dates from 1800 BC, and at its centre stands the ancient parish church. So the site has played host to religious activities for some 1400 years.

The Norman church is built of knapped flint, flint which has been chopped in half with the freshly cut surface showing. Inside, the walls have lost much of their original plaster finish as the roof has collapsed, allowing the weather to take its toll.

But why a Christian church on a pagan site? Well, the answer is quite simple, early Christian missionaries found it easier to convert our ancestors by preaching to them on sites which already had a religious significance to them, albeit pagan.

Dorset's Egyptian connection can be found on the lawn of **Kingston Lacy House**, owned by the National Trust. A tall stone column called the Philae Needle, an ancient Egyptian obelisk, stands there. Prior to 1822 it was assumed that hieroglyphs were merely symbols until Jean Francis Champollion learnt to decipher them, using the Philae needle and the Rosetta stone, discovering that these symbols were letters which could be read.

So you could call it the column which helped to explain the meaning of Egyptian hieroglyphs. This site was selected and the first stone laid in 1827 by the Duke of Wellington.

The inscription around the base explains that 'William John Banks Esq M.P. eldest son of Henry Banks Esq M.P. caused this obelisk and the pedestal from which it had fallen to be removed from the Island of Philae beyond the first cataract and brought this platform, the stepped base from the nuns of Hierassycaminon in Nubia. The granite used was brought from the remains of Lepis Magna in Africa and was given for that purpose by his Majesty King George IV.'

The inscriptions on the obelisk and pedestal record their dedication to King Ptolemy Euergetes II and his two queens who authorised the priest of Isis to erect them about 150 BC as a perpetual memorial of exemption from taxation. What a splendid reason for a memorial!

The Conduit at Sherborne – a 'little gem' that has seen many uses over its six centuries but has now been carefully restored.

There's another bit of Egypt in the heart of Dorset – unique is the only way to describe the Tutankhamun Exhibition at **Dorchester**. The brain child of Dr. Michael Ridley, it is a complete and faithful reproduction of the finding of, and treasures in King Tutankhamun's tomb. Life-size figures of the main participants of the find, Howard Carter, Lord Carnavon and others 'play out' the finding of the tomb and you can share the experience with them. Every part of the tomb is authentic and to scale. Music, commentary and actors' and actresses' voices take you through the whole story from the boy king's reign to Carter's discovery.

For me the most unusual thing about the museum, for museum it really is, is the aroma. The smells of the place have been recreated and the aromatic scent is exactly as it was when Carter opened the tomb. You can even buy a packet of the smell to take home with you!

In an adjoining gallery are all the treasures of the tomb faithfully reproduced; taking pride of place is the famous gold mask every bit as enigmatic as the original. It too is made of gold and actually took 18 months to make, whereas the original, we are reliably informed, took Egyptian craftsmen a mere 70 days!

Unique in a different way is **Woodsford Castle** – it is probably one of the largest thatched buildings in the country and certainly the only thatched castle in England. Resembling a fortified manor house it was granted a licence to crenellate in 1337 by Edward III. Much of the building is of the original 14th century stonework, although there are a few more recent additions. The inside includes two large halls, a queen's chamber, a guards' chamber and an oratory. A truly unique building of which Dorset should be proud.

It seems fitting to end this swift tour of the county with some refreshment. The Smiths Arms at **Godmanstone** is unusual rather than strange. It claims to be the smallest pub in England. Once the local smithy, this tiny stone building, with its enormous thatched roof, was visited by Charles II during his escape from the battle of Worcester in 1651. He asked the blacksmith for a glass of ale. The reply was prompt 'I have no licence, Sir'. On hearing this the King immediately granted him a licence and there has been an inn here ever since. The inn sign, looking almost too large for the size of the tiny pub, depicts the story of the royal visit.

Inside it is minute, being a mere 39 feet (12m) long, 11½ feet

Life-size figures play out the finding of the tomb in the Valley of the Kings. Music, voices, even smells, take visitors through the experience.

The boy king – remembered in a 'little bit of Egypt' in Dorset.

(3.5m) wide and 12 feet (3.6m) high with the actual bar only 19½ feet (6m) by 10 feet (3m). This delightful little pub is understandably very popular and visitors over the years must have been eternally grateful that King Charles II's horse threw a shoe here in this particular Dorset smithy. It really is a pleasure as well as a unique experience to take refreshment at England's tiniest hostelry.

... visitors over the years must have been eternally grateful that King Charles II's horse threw a shoe here ...

Introducing ...

BARNEY CAMFIELD, who lives at Exeter, is not only a frequent visitor to Dorset, he has a deep affinity with Dorset – and often lectures at Sherborne and Bryanston.

Barney – christened Bernard Jesse Oliver – Camfield was born at Barters Farm, eight miles south of Salisbury and has always retained a love of farming and country life. After service in the Commandos during the second world war, he was invalided out in 1945 and became involved in earning his living in films and television. After a study in psychology though, this has become his primary interest, and has become well-known for his work in the field of psychosomatic medicine and healing.

Mr Camfield has been minister of Moretonhampstead Unitarian Church since 1967, is Chairman of the Westcountry Natural Healing Fellowship and founded Moreton Healing Fellowship with branches in the South and West.

His previous contributions to the Bossiney list are Healing, Harmony & Health and Loving, Laughing & Living and a chapter in Dorset Mysteries.

Here he explores ley lines in Dorset, earth energy lines known to the Chinese as Dragon lines.

An old photograph taken among the Purbeck Hills.

'All things by immortal power,
Near or far, hiddenly
To each other linkèd are,
That thou canst not stir a flower
Without troubling of a star.'

Francis Thompson 1859-1907

LEY LINES AND DRAGON LINES

Barney Camfield

The term ley lines was first defined by Alfred Watkins in his book *The Old Straight Track*. 'Ley' is an obsolete word meaning island. Not just islands in the sea but high points or clear observation points from which one could see the 'lay of the land'.

There are four or five different types of lines loosely referred to as ley lines but some not exactly just straight tracks. And some are so wide that they have been redefined as 'corridors'.

There is no doubt that many were, in the days before roads and signposts, routes concerned with travel. Some of these may be associated with earth energy but the strong indications are that there are many ley lines which were not just travel routes. They are earth energy lines – which the Chinese refer to as Dragon lines. A romantic description perhaps but it finds favour in my mind; in part I think because of the strong – yet subtle – power which these lines have.

However man has interfered with these earth energy lines, sometimes unthinkingly but often deliberately so, by gnostics – those with the ageless knowledge – using them. Just as agriculturalists have diverted water from rivers and streams to water land and thus benefit crops so the wise ones tapped the lines for the same purpose, to benefit crops and also sentient life. By building earth circles and erecting standing stones, these knowers and sensitives of the day diverted, guided and strengthened the earth energies flowing along energy lines to provide extra energy of the right type to improve the health of the crops, their animals and themselves.

Harking back to Arthurian days about 475A.D., one of my colleagues in regression saw a point where these energy lines crossed. 'It looked like a grid if you were able to see it; grids of light,' says Arthur.

I wrote in *Dorset Mysteries* in more detail of Arthur (King Arthur as he is popularly known) and I told of some of the mystical sites in Dorset with which Arthur is associated. His birth place and his burial place and also the place of worship where earth energy was concentrated to focus the ley line energy at Knowlton Rings. Here St Mellion (Merlin) and other Celtic Christian priests drew upon this energy to strengthen Arthur, his chiefs, their warriors and their weapons. Knowlton Circles is one point of a triangle composed of Wimborne Minster, the region of Buzbury Rings and Knowlton Circles.

Knowlton Circles is an example of an energy spring or geyser which has been strengthened or organised by man-made earthworks which, according to expert dowsers, acted much as radio or television aerials do when receiving and transmitting radio waves. The earth energy aerial consisted of the circular rings on the ground with the height of the mounds and the depths of the associated ditches carefully measured in order to trap the energy of a particular wave length. The henge or standing stones also directed or changed the direction and strength of the energy flow.

Knowlton Rings, 6½ miles north of Wimborne, is a recognised sacred circle and myself and others who are more psychically sensitive than me are aware of its power.

This centre lined up with a site in Wimborne upon which an early Celtic Christian church was erected just to one side of where the Minster now stands. The third point of the triangle is Buzbury Rings near Tarrant Keyneston, which lies astride the Wimborne Blandford road. Part of it is incorporated in a golf course! It has been classified as a hillfort; though this has been questioned. The energy here is scattered because of the changes and the road running through it but it still has power. I am very much of the opinion that other sites classified as hill forts were indeed energy centres which later became defended settlements. Maiden Castle at Winterbourne St Martins for example.

The circular rituals at these sites – such as the Nine Stones, an old Celtic temple near Winterbourne Abbas – are very similar to those taught by Pythagoras and still used throughout the world by followers of his spiritual teachings.

Bob Sephton, until recently, was a senior executive in the power industry occupied with generating electricity. For over ten years he has also been deeply concerned with the subtler etheric energies

Knowlton Church and circles – a source of energy whose power is said to be sensed by those attuned to the ancient rhythms.

Barney Camfield on the supernatural trail in Dorset.

involved in man, nature and in energised ley lines; ever since he found that he had the ability to dowse. He is also a member of the British Society of Dowsers.

One summer's day in 1981, not long after the family had taken up residence in a village not far from Wimborne, he and his daughter were dowsing on the front lawn, examining an energy line which came through the bungalow and across the lawn. He discovered variations in the flow which then led to the discovery of the remains of a small stone circle. None of the stones of about four feet in height were still standing but Bob has since either recovered the stones or replaced them with suitable fresh ones – which is a story in itself! – and now has his own stone circle of five stones. It is a pentagon really, Bob says.

Five streams of energy come into and out of the circle and in his work of rebuilding a deal of care had to be taken to obviate 'geopathic stress' on individuals. He says: 'In the case of our bungalow I had found that too many positive energy lines were passing through the end bedrooms, whereas negative energy lines were required.'

Bob also found that a well had been situated where the dining room now is and that water had been drawn from it for healing purposes.

Geopathic stress is felt by humans (probably felt by plants and animals as well; but they can't so easily tell us what is wrong) due to earth energies of some kind – mostly, apparently, yin type energies. (Yin = feminine; Yang = masculine).

A few years ago I was asked to deal with a depressed patient in Dorset and, to cut a long story short, eventually found that an energy line was passing through the corner of the house with the intensity greater in the upper floor where it was flowing through the patient's bedroom. Changing the placing of the bed did not help much, but changing rooms certainly did while a spell of over a month away from the house had a splendid effect.

In all fields of energy, including that within our body, there are negative and positive aspects and flows and counterflows. This applies to earth energy lines also.

According to Bob there is evidence of rearrangement of sites over the years. 'Sometimes the whole system was re-organised. Instead of lots of small sites, major systems were built. Knowlton Circles, Badbury Rings and Fisbury Rings for example. The small stone circles then became distribution points hanging like pendants from the main system. The evidence I have is that the earthworks in this area were fully energised by around 1500 B.C.'

He strongly advocates NOT buying a house under or even near an overhead power line. Another friend of mine who is an electrical engineer in Gloucestershire is having a great problem dealing with a customer whose TV sets, electric cooker, vacuum cleaner etc are constantly blowing up and have to be replaced and repaired. He swears that it is because the customer's house is situated extremely close to overhead power lines.

From our Arthurian research Mellion (Merlin) and his priests and priestesses were aware of dragon lines and put them to good use during the days of Arthur and their battles against the Saxons. Michael Williams has, on a number of occasions interviewed '. . . a brown eyed housewife' who does not wish to be identified. She has regressed to apparent past lives on hundreds of occasions in my

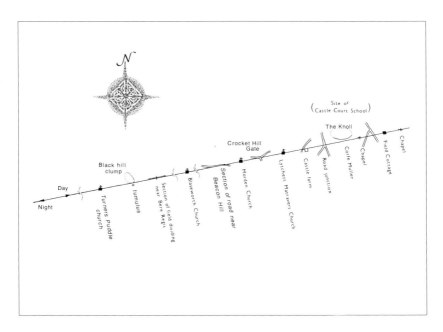

Bob Sephton charts the line of a typical energy flow.

presence. Many times – and she was very reluctant to admit to it at first – as Arturus, King Arthur. In the Bossiney book, *Strange Somerset Stories* Michael has written a chapter on Arthur's connections in Somerset. In his presence she regressed to observe her life as Arthur. Michael asked if Cadbury was important.

'. . . *It is a very, very important place. I can 'see' that this particular fortress was very important to Arthur because it was a link in his fortress chain. I can pick up this information by viewing the area from above, as if I were in an aircraft. What I 'see' is that there is a particular ley line going from Glastonbury to Cadbury, and from Cadbury it links around right up to the Severn estuary, going across the river to the south eastern tip of Wales and there is another centre there. If you can understand this – that travel was much easier if you used those ley lines. It was speedy to use all the energy flow and you got from A to B much better than if you were off it. So they were used for communication in all sorts of ways.*'

Bob Sephton says that each site where the earth energy lines were brought into use by earthworks and henges was in the charge of a priest or priestess. 'If one site was yin, then as far as it was able to be arranged, the next one would be yang. This maintains a yin-yang balance. Buzbury Rings between Blandford and Badbury Rings was yang. Badbury Rings and Knowlton were yin. Woolsbarrow Rings were yang.'

I was surprised that Knowlton was yin because those present at the ceremonies during apparent past lives in Arthurian times were chiefs and their senior warriors while senior priests carried out the rituals. There were no females present at these times. But I have dowsed and it is certainly yin now and the indications confirm that it was yin in the days of Arthur.

Ley energy lines are often associated with hill tops and these hill tops are often associated with the Archangel Michael. On the day we were welcomed to Bob and Helen Sephton's home we finished up in the early evening heading towards Abbotsbury. Gereint, who was with us, had been informed that somewhere in Dorset there was 'a Michael hill in sight of the sea'. so we'd followed our intuitive noses in this direction towards the Hardy Monument. I didn't

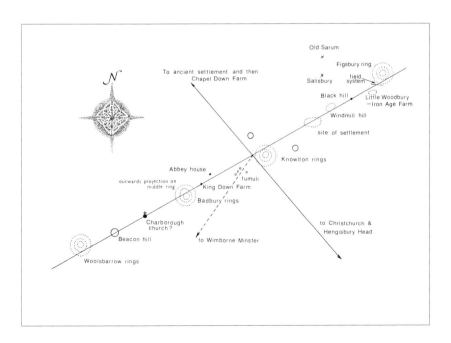

A major system of large stone circles.

particularly care for this memorial to Admiral Sir Thomas Hardy, once Nelson's Flag Captain, it so reminds me of a factory chimney! But we parked the car nearby to stretch our legs and walked around behind it. It was then I 'saw' that this was it – this was the Michael hill! A veritable geyser of energy. I 'saw' two light lines – energy lines – one streaming to the northwest and the other streaming to the northeast. On checking with a map I found that one led straight to Glastonbury and Cadbury Camp and the other to Stonehenge. I said nothing of what I had 'seen' but asked Gereint to get comfortable, look back to about 1000 B.C. and gradually come forward in time. The essence of his findings was that here was an energy point at which war gods had been worshipped and invoked. The gods changed and the temples changed as the tribes changed. But at one time during the Celtic Christian times there was a temple to the chief of God's defenders, the Archangel Michael.

I found two other factors of interest later. Dowsing showed me that the width of the ley energy line there was nearly ten yards. Also I 'saw' it streaming out across the channel and on checking the direction on the map I saw that it linked up with Mont St Michel in France, another Michael point. I 'saw' too, ships crossing from France to England along this line. Probably someone on board was using psychic sight together perhaps with a crystal or two.

A few weeks ago, Michael, the farmer friend of mine, told me that he was going to Bournemouth for the weekend. I asked him if he could possibly go out of his way a little on the return journey and see what he got at the Hardy Memorial. I said nothing of other findings and Michael had never before visited the monument. Here are his notes which he gave me later.

'I am standing below Hardy's monument. It is evening and the sun is setting. Below me everything is gently touched by the gold; the bluebells, the fir trees, the distant hills and the sea. I feel an extraordinary sense of power, of energy.

'As I relax and meditate time changes. Now I am back several thousand years. I see a temple – built not for public worship but for tapping into and using the power, the energy that is in this area. To increase the mystical abilities of the priests – and others approved by them.

'The temple was strangely shaped. Round, with nine pillars surrounding it and five pillars within. There was one main chamber

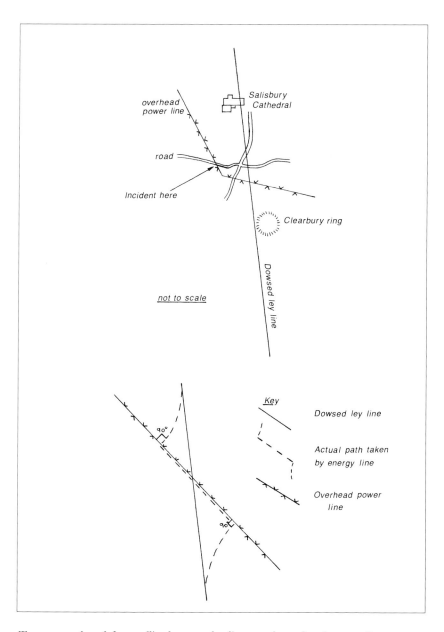

Two examples of the conflict between ley lines and overhead power lines.

and, almost hidden at the back, was a small inner chamber, a "holy of holies". The temple had a flat roof and I sense it was built with pure, godly motives.

'A time change. The temple has had a pointed roof built on it, reminiscent of a steeple. To bring holy power down to those below? It somehow reminds me of a birdcage!

'Again, a time change. And a change in atmosphere too. I see robed figures in black. A little sinister. I feel that this group of people have taken over the temple to plug into the power for their own desires, for egotistical selfish reasons. It is a period of darkness and fear. I 'know' that both good and bad groups were aware of the energy and vitality of not just this hill but of the ley lines in the area and were used to the harnessing of it. Energy which could be used for good or not so good according to the motives of the users. As can so many other gifts of God!'

Michael was most interested when I told him of what Gereint and I had found including the 'sight' of the black period. And now Arthur confirms the findings too.

Well – I wish I had space and time to tell you more but . . . why not get your map and pendulum out and find yourself some energy ley lines? We'd be interested to know how you get on. If you want more information concerning the subject get in touch with your local "Fountain" group or contact the Secretary of the British Society of Dowsers, Sycamore Cottage, Tamley Lane, Hastingleigh, Ashford, Kent TN25 5HW, who will put you in touch with your local society.

Hardy's Monument. ▶

56

Introducing ...

FELICITY YOUNG is a Cornish-based painter who lives at Tintagel, North Cornwall with her husband Ian, daughter Hazel and dog Arthur. She lived in Somerset for more than twenty years and still makes regular visits to the county. She was educated at Lord Digby's Grammar School, Sherborne, Dorset.

Since 1984 she has contributed 250 illustrations for a whole range of Bossiney titles, covering six areas: Cornwall, Devon, Somerset, Avon, Dorset and Wiltshire – and she recently did a radio broadcast on the craft of illustrating books. A member of The British Horse Society, she rides regularly and is a riding instructor at The Tall Trees Riding Stables near Camelford. She also teaches yoga.

In 1989 Felicity made her debut as a Bossiney author, contributing a chapter on Lawrence of Arabia in Dorset Mysteries. *Then in 1990 came her first book* Curiosities of Exmoor, *a fascinating tour in words and pictures showing that Exmoor has its fair share of rarities and wonders. Now she recalls Charlotte Bryant, a small-time prostitute accused of murdering her husband.*

MURDER BY POISON

Felicity Young

MURDER is invariably a strange business. The idyllic county of Dorset is an unlikely setting for such a crime. However, in December 1935, in the hamlet of Coombe in the parish of Castleton, a murder was committed.

The outcome of the trial was the hanging of Charlotte Bryant, found guilty of poisoning her husband, Fred, with arsenic. More than fifty years on, doubt still remains as to the accuracy of vital evidence which sealed poor Charlotte's fate. If it had not been for the fact that she had confided in her 'best' friend Lucy Ostler and given herself away, the case may well have gone down in history as a grave miscarriage of justice. As it was, Charlotte, a simple girl, had callously and cruelly attempted to poison Frederick John Bryant on several other occasions and as good as confessed to Lucy what she had done.

Charlotte McHugh was born in Londonderry in 1903. In her youth she was a pretty girl; she turned to prostitution at a very early age, realising it was her only hope of making a living. She was unable to read or write and knew that her body would always be her only asset. She met her husband Fred whilst he was serving in Ireland as a military policeman with the Dorset Regiment. They eloped in October 1922, were married at Mells in Somerset and began their life together at Nether Compton near Taunton. In 1934, just one year before Fred's agonising death, they moved with their children to live in a small cottage at Coombe Farm in Dorset.

Here Fred took a job as farm labourer. He was a dull, taciturn kind of a fellow. Marrying a soldier may have seemed glamorous to Charlotte, but a mere farm labourer could not give her the love and excitement she craved. She went back to her old ways, earning a few extra shillings for herself, frequenting all the pubs and inns in the area.

Fred never asked any questions as to where her money came from or about her numerous relationships. Did he not wonder how she managed to buy cream and tins of salmon from his meagre wages of £1.18s.6d and how she managed to afford to drink at the local hostelries every night? Perhaps he was too simple to notice or maybe he did not want to upset the family home, such as it was. Whichever the reason, through no fault of his own he was to meet a horrible, painful end at the hand of his wife.

Charlotte became besotted with a gipsy horse-dealer named Leonard Parsons. It was this infatuation that drove her to poison her unwitting husband. She could think of nothing but the disposal of this dull man so that she could run away with her lover for a life of excitement. She did not think twice about committing murder – it seemed a satisfactory conclusion to a girl of simple thoughts and little intelligence. Charlotte knew nothing about poisons and it took three attempts before she finally achieved her aim. Three times Fred suffered horribly, each time to recover and be subjected again to Charlotte's wicked deeds. By the time she had succeeded in killing Fred, her lover Parsons had fled from the cottage where he had been lodging with Charlotte, Fred and the children. He returned to the gipsy site at Weston-super-Mare where he already

The idyllic county of Dorset ...

had a common-law wife waiting for him.

It remains a mystery as to whether he had become suspicious of Fred's unaccountable illnesses or whether he was driven away by the constant string of paying 'customers' which Charlotte brought to the house. She was reputed to have asked Parsons: 'What would you do if I was a widow? Would you marry me?' Perhaps this caused him to leave so suddenly in November 1935 without a word. Many onlookers at the trial would have made Parsons a prime suspect for Fred's murder but for the fact the final attempt at poisoning came a month after Parsons had fled.

It is a wonder that Parsons found Charlotte attractive at all. The years of prostitution and child-bearing had taken their toll and she was by no means the pretty Irish maid of her youth. Toothless, haggard and unwashed, her hair wound in an unflattering style into two tight buns and worn about her ears like earmuffs, it could only have been the glint in her eye that attracted the likes of Parsons.

Charlotte emerged at her trial as a sad pathetic figure, but this diminutive woman had attempted to poison her husband not once but several times, watching, unmoved as he writhed in agony. She thought only of her gipsy lover; she had not the intelligence to see the consequences of her actions.

Charlotte kept her house, a small semi-detached for which Fred paid a weekly rent of three shillings in much the same way she cared for her own appearance. It was filthy and dishevelled. Where some cottagers planted flowers in their gardens Charlotte used hers as a rubbish tip, throwing out the empty bottles and tins, a practice that eventually led to her being unmasked as a poisoner. It was on to this heap that she tossed the half-burnt tin of arsenic. The family lived in squalor; Charlotte's upbringing gave her no inclination to provide a clean and comfortable home for her husband and children. They had to live the only way she knew.

Fred first suffered acute stomach pains in May 1935. Dr McCarthy of Sherborne diagnosed it as 'gastric trouble', with Fred's medical history of dysentery this seemed a safe diagnosis. Other attacks soon followed, one in August, another in November at the time that Parsons left. Finally on December 21 Fred became mortally ill. He was admitted by Dr McCarthy to the Yeatman Hospital in Sherborne. He had often refused to go to hospital in the past claiming it was a place that people never came out of alive. This

Charlotte Bryant's cottage.

time though he had very little say in the matter as he was seriously ill. His prediction was correct; the next day, with Charlotte standing at his bedside he died. It must have been a blessed relief from the intense suffering which Charlotte had inflicted upon him.

Dr McCarthy had by this time become suspicious of Fred's mysterious attacks. He refused to sign the death certificate and ordered a post mortem. Arsenic was found in every organ of the body analysed and it was clear how Fred had died. The cottage at Coombe was thoroughly searched by the police and arsenic, or traces of it, were found in several places. This finding was actually not very surprising as arsenic abounds in the Dorset soil and it could have been brought into the house by Fred himself on his boots. Evidence had to be found to prove that Charlotte had bought arsenic. A container was found and on February 10 1936 Charlotte was arrested and charged with the murder of her husband.

She was brought to her trial at Dorchester from Holloway. It must have been a frightening experience for her, a long way from any familiar faces and completely out of her depth. Her fate was in the hands of the jury at the Dorset Summer Assizes. A curious public watched, intrigued by the case and eager to get a glimpse of the 'foreigner' accused of brutal murder. The courtroom was filled to capacity to hear the indictment read by Justice MacKinnon. The charge was 'On divers dates between May 1 and December 22 1935, at Coombe in the parish of Castleton, in the county of Dorset, she did feloniously, wilfully and with malice aforethought administer poison, to wit arsenic, to Frederick John Bryant, and there did kill and murder him.'

Charlotte appeared to be overwhelmed by her surroundings, unable to grasp the seriousness of the situation. Did she perhaps believe that the testimony of her young children would sway the jury or that her only friend, Lucy Ostler, might speak up for her? In fact Lucy was there to testify against her, relating the truth about Charlotte's premeditated actions. She could expect no pity from this court despite her pitiful appearance.

Leonard Parsons, a distinctive man with blue eyes and grey-tinged, once fair hair, took the stand. Describing himself as a horse-dealer he told how he met Charlotte some time before in Sherborne. He told the court of his love affair with her and how he came to lodge with the family at Coombe but had to leave suddenly in November 1935. It came to light that Parsons was the father of Charlotte's youngest child but he did not seem to place much importance on this and was not bothered about leaving the child behind when he returned to his camp, declaring it would be better off with its mother. It was on May 13 1935, the court was told, that Charlotte and Parsons had gone out drinking taking the eldest child with them. Fred had returned from work, having eaten a packed lunch prepared for him by Charlotte, suffering from severe stomach pains. The next door neighbour, Mrs Staunton, had gone to his assistance and put him to bed.

By some fluke he survived Charlotte's first attempt at murder. When she returned home she was alarmed to find him still alive. She would have to try all over again, and try again she did but with no more success than the first attempt.

Next to take the stand was Charlotte's only friend Lucy. As she began to speak it became clear that any hope Charlotte may have had was drifting away with this young girl's testimony. Lucy had become friends with Charlotte just before her second attempt to dispose of Fred. Charlotte admitted that she was in love with Parsons and that her youngest child was his. She had even invited Lucy to sleep in the same room with herself and her husband and had 'allowed' her to be witness to the deed of administering the poison. She had drawn Lucy's attention to a mysterious green tin and declared 'I must get rid of that'. On Boxing Day she had tried to burn it but failed to light the fire. Calling for Lucy's help, between them they managed to pull out all the rubbish from the grate and throw it out into the garden. Amongst it was the tin which the police later discovered to have contained arsenic. It was identified as being similar to one sold to a woman by a chemist in Yeovil on the afternoon of December 21. Although the chemist could not identify Charlotte as the woman in question, despite an identification parade in which both Charlotte and Lucy appeared, the court still felt this was valuable evidence.

Charlotte sat silently as her 'friend' betrayed her. Her world seemed to be falling apart and she was all alone, her only friend lost beyond the point of no return, revealing all her darkest secrets. She told how, on the night of December 21 while sleeping in Fred and Charlotte's room, she awoke to see the shadowy figure of Charlotte trying to force Fred to drink a cup of Oxo and how within minutes he was violently ill and vomiting. Lucy had seen the murderess crouching over the poor man, watching his agony, appearing to be the ministering angel but in truth the angel of death.

A little light relief entered the courtroom for a brief moment when two gipsy women gave evidence on behalf of Parsons. The younger, a Mrs Loveridge claimed she had four children by him and he had lived with her at the gipsy encampment at Weston-super-Mare for some time. She knew he had been lodging with the Bryants but was not bothered by the relationship as she was as near to his legal wife as possible and knew he would return. She wore brightly coloured clothes but did not have a gipsy look about her. Her mother, Mrs Penfold, however, was a true Romany with high cheekbones and dark eyes. In each ear she wore a heavily jewelled earring which glinted and sparkled in the shafts of sunlight. With their departure the courtroom became very grim and sombre, almost as though their leaving had taken the life from the place.

The senior analyst to the Home Office, Dr Roche Lynch, was next in the witness box. It was his controversial statement that referred to the abnormally high proportion of arsenic, 149 parts per million in the ashes of Charlotte's grate indicating, he declared, that something containing arsenic had been burnt there. He virtually put the noose around her neck. The green tin which Lucy had identified and the tin sold by the chemist fitted neatly into that part of the jigsaw. The jury had little deliberating to do. Charlotte's web of intrigue was slowly being unravelled, a web this seemingly innocent woman had woven about her, and now, thread by thread, it was disintegrating, plunging her to certain execution on the gallows.

Charlotte seemed already a condemned woman when she took the stand, but she could raise a smile when she saw the blue coat which the police had found contained traces of arsenic in its pockets. In her ignorance she insisted that she had not worn the coat on the day she was accused of murdering Fred and trying it on, hoping to prove her innocence, she showed the court that it was too short in the sleeves. This little exhibition was to no avail as there was no doubt that the coat had contained arsenic and that it was her coat. Charlotte's simple mind could not grasp this; it did not matter one jot that she had not worn it on that particular day, being her garment she might have placed the poison in the pocket at any time.

With all the evidence heard, Charlotte had to wait for the final summing up before she knew what her fate would be. Three hours she waited, three long hours, while the judge went through his summation and another hour of torment before the jury returned with its verdict. Perhaps this painful delay was justice in itself for the dreadful suffering she had caused Fred. The judge dismissed the possibility that Fred may have tried to poison himself, one attempt might have been possible but certainly not on three occasions. After suffering such agony once it seemed highly unlikely he would have allowed himself to suffer again. The judge said the accused was the only person living in the house on each occasion, Parsons and Lucy

The face of a murderess – taken from a contemporary newspaper account of the trial.

Ostler were there some of the time, but not consistently, so could be dismissed as suspects. Charlotte was the only person who had the motive and the opportunity to commit the crime.

The jury returned a verdict of guilty. The judge placed the Black Cap upon his head and passed sentence: 'Charlotte Bryant, after a long and careful trial you have been found guilty of the murder of your husband by killing him by a long and painful death. It only remains for me to discharge my duty. That is that you be taken from this place, to a lawful place of execution and hanged by the neck until you are dead, and buried in the precincts of the prison. May the Lord have mercy on your soul.'

At last Charlotte broke down and wept, not tears of regret but tears of fear as the reality of the situation finally dawned on her.

She was a heartless creature who had taken a macabre pleasure in watching her helpless husband as he writhed in agony. She had experimented with the deadly dose of arsenic until she finally succeeded in killing him, just as if she was ridding herself of an unwanted dog. She had no feelings of remorse for what she had done. It was not easy for her to be furtive or secretive. It was not in her nature, she was basically simple and ignorant, and this was her undoing.

Even though she was so obviously guilty there did appear one glaring error which cast doubt on the credibility of the trial. The judge had stated that it had been a 'long and careful trial' but had it? Professor William A. Bone, of the Imperial College of Science and Technology, disagreed with Dr Lynch's statement relating to the amount of arsenic found in the ashes of Charlotte's grate. Professor Bone pointed out that household coal could sometimes contain as much as 1000 parts per million of arsenic and in actual fact the reading of 149 parts per million was a very low reading. This directly refuted Lucy Ostler's statement that the tin containing the poison had been burnt in the fire. If this had been the case the reading would have been much higher. A shadow of doubt had been cast upon what had seemed a clear cut case. Dr Lynch had made an incredible mistake. It was his evidence that had been instrumental in sending Charlotte to the gallows and now it appeared to be totally inaccurate.

The case went to the Appeals Judges but to no avail, they would not reverse the decision. In their eyes Charlotte was guilty of wilful murder and nothing could save her from death. Appeals were made to the Home Secretary and a petition launched by Mrs Van de Elst, a fierce opponent of capital punishment, in the hope of securing a reprieve for Charlotte but all this was useless. On July 15 1936 at Exeter Prison she was hanged.

This was indeed an intriguing case: a woman convicted and hanged on such flimsy evidence. Perhaps the court was influenced by her character and the fact that she was a prostitute and in their eyes a women of low morals who got what she deserved. She was not 'one of them' having come from Ireland. The murder of prostitutes is not uncommon. Some believe Jack the Ripper was in fact a Dorset man; but murder by a prostitute is rare and this particular crime gripped the attention of Dorset people.

Introducing ...

TOM PERROTT, who was born in Bridport, is a former Secretary of the Society of Dorset Men. He now lives in London and is Chairman of The Ghost Club, founded in 1862, whose members have included Sir Arthur Conan Doyle, Charles Dickens and Dennis Wheatley. He is an investigator and lectur-er for the Society of Psychical Research – and was co-author of Ghosts of Dorset, Devon & Somerset. *In his debut for Bossiney, Tom Perrott writes about strange features of his native county.*

A MEDLEY OF STRANGE DORSET FACTS

Tom Perrott

WHEN one considers the multiplicity of curiosities and mysteries that are to be found in the County of Dorset, it is not difficult to see how Thomas Hardy found it to be such a fertile source of information and inspiration for the writing of his celebrated Wessex novels.

Over the past two or three decades, phenomena as exemplified by the alleged sightings of Unidentified Flying Objects and the sudden appearance of strange Corn Crop Circles, have received a great deal of publicity in West Country media, but few people are aware that an account of the sighting of a UFO in the area of Cranborne, appeared in the September 1738 issue of *The Gentleman's Magazine*. It was reported '*that on the 29th of last month at five in the afternoon, was seen near this place a surprising Meteor, or Phenomenon in the Sky to ye North East, the sun shining bright. It first appeared as Fire bursting from behind a Cloud, out of which fire issued a light glowing Ball, with a train of flame behind it, which quickly disappeared. The same was seen at Wells in Somersetshire; also at Tapton in Derbyshire about the same time, it did not come from behind a Cloud, for the sky was quite free from Clouds, and the sun shin'd very clear, it appeared like a cone of Fire, which terminated in a sharp point, with a bright Nucleus or a Ball at its thicker end, which seem'd to burst and go away in a great Flame. It was about South East. At Reading and 15 miles round (the same time) an astonishing Noise was heard in the Air, when it was quite serene. The Crack which was very sudden and violent was succeeded by a rumbling Noise for the Space of a Minute. This Phenomenon by its Description from different parts, perfectly agrees with what happened in the Month of March 1719, and was very dreadful and Surprizing to the Western Parts of England, and is that sort of Meteor which Naturalists call Draco Volens, or, a Flying Dragon*'.

Another strange phenomenon sometimes encountered in Dorset

is that of the Singing Sands, and the melodies have often been heard on the beach between South Haven Point and Studland. Having disembarked from the Sandbanks Ferry, one can often find within a distance of a hundred yards or more, that one's footsteps have been accompanied by the melodies of singing sands.

The patches of sand are usually to be found above a recent high water mark where the sand is not too dry or powdery, and not as wet as it would be lower down the beach. Sometimes the sounds produced are louder on some days than on others, and the areas thus motified vary in size.

The sound produced resembles that produced when finger-nails are rubbed on the cover of a book, and is said to increase after hard scuffling. Sometimes these sounds can be created when one lightly flicks the surface of the sand with a piece of wood or a stick.

Many theories have been put forward in an attempt to explain this phenomenon. One suggests that as the grains of sand are round and polished and of a more or less uniform size, the vibrations produced are of the same frequency and so combine to produce a volume of sound sufficient to be audible.

Another theory refers to the amount of moisture present in the sand, as it does not 'sing' if it is either too wet or too dry. The singing is loudest and best when the sand is drying off after having been recently wet.

When taken captive and forcibly removed from their Dorset shore, the sands soon lapse into a sullen silence.

Most parish churches in this county are dedicated to particular saints, but few churches can claim to be custodians for the relics of the subjects of their dedication.

One exception to this is the delightful little Church of St. Candida and Holy Cross, in the village of Whitechurch Canonicorum, resting peacefully in the sleepy Marshwood Vale. In mediaeval times it was considered that if people went on a pilgrimage to the resting places of the remains of their patron saints, their virtue would be assured and very often they would be miraculously cured of the many conditions that at that time their flesh often found itself heir to. St Candida or St Wita, a martyred saint, believed to have been of Breton origin, was traditionally believed to have been laid to rest at Whitechurch Canonicorum. Accordingly her shrine became a place of pilgrimage for many cen-

An old photograph of Studland Bay where the sands can be heard singing ...

turies and in the openings of her altar tomb, handkerchiefs and pieces of material were often placed, in the hope that they would become impregnated with the healing powers of the Saint, when they would later be carried away and eventually brought into contact with the persons for whom the healing powers had been sought.

In April of the year 1900, when certain renovations were being carried out in the Church, a leaden casket was revealed, bearing an inscription with the words HIC RE QUECT RLIQE SCE WITE (Here rest the remains of St Wita or Candida). When the casket was opened it was found to contain the bones of a small woman. Even to this day the wild periwinkles which grow in such profusion on nearby Stonebarrow Hill are called St Candida's Eyes and in the neighbouring village of Morcombelake, is to be found St Candida's Well, the water of which is said to possess curative properties, particularly for sore eyes.

A similar event also took place at Shaftesbury Abbey. The abbey

The sacred well near Whitchurch Canonicorum.

The north transept of the church showing St Wite's shrine. ▶

was one of Dorset's greatest ecclesiastical glories. Originally established by King Alfred it had accumulated great wealth over the years, in fact it used to be said that if 'the Abbot of Glaston (Glastonbury) married the Abbess of Shaston (Shaftesbury) their combined wealth would have been greater than that of the King of England'. A century after its founding, the abbey jealously guarded the mortal remains of the young King, Edward the Martyr, who was treacherously murdered by his stepmother, while hunting in the vicinity of Corfe Castle.

The Abbey became a place of pilgrimage, for those who wished to visit the shrine of the martyred king. At the dissolution of the monasteries, the tomb was destroyed, the remains of the king appeared to have been lost forever and the once stately abbey became a vast ruin. Many excavations were carried out on the site, and in 1930, when digging was being done on the site of the former high altar, a casket was unearthed and when opened was found to contain – the bones of a young man.

The graceful lines of historical Wimborne Minster never fail to attract the many tourists travelling through the ancient town, on their way to the coastal resorts of the West. Those who have entered its sacred portals may have noticed in the South Chapel, a highly coloured sarcophagus, which contains the remains of one Anthony Ettricke. Ettricke was a lawyer, an eccentric and a great friend of John Aubrey, the celebrated antiquary. He firmly believed that he would depart this life in the year 1691, because these figures have the strange quality of reading the same, even when turned upside down. Accordingly he had that date printed on his tomb, but an alteration had eventually to be made, as he did not die until 1703. For some strange reason Ettricke gave instructions that he would neither be buried in the church, nor in the churchyard and by using his legal cunning, he instructed that he should be buried in the wall. His wishes were followed to the letter, as a result of which, he has come to be known as 'the man in the wall.'

When the foundations of important buildings were to be laid, it was customary to place a sealed casket in the masonry to show future generations some of the everyday objects of the time. A relic

St Wite's parish church of Whitchurch Canonicorum.

box of this kind was introduced inside one of the piers of a Dorset church in 1911. A label attached indicated the contents included 'a man's skull, a horse's skull, a parish magazine and the vicar's appendix preserved in spirits.'

The study of epitaphs and inscriptions on gravestones in Dorset can often be most rewarding and it is fascinating to sample the examples of rustic humour that have often been composed on the most solemn occasions. A former rector of Marnhull sought to immortalise the memory of his clerk John Warren, who died in 1752 at the ripe old age of ninety-four with the following words, which appeared on an inscription in the church:-

> Here under this stone
> Lie Ruth and old John
> Who smoked all his life
> And so did his wife;
> And now there's no doubt
> But their pipes are both out.
> Be it said without joke
> That life is but smoke
> Though you live to fourscore
> 'Tis a whiff and no more.

How the members of the anti-smoking lobby, so active today would have relished these words of wisdom.

Although vampire stories are fairly rare in this country, one true one centres around the once mighty Eastbury House, at Tarrant Gunville, not far from Blandford Forum. This house was considered to have been one of the most superb and grand in the county, and had belonged to that vain and lecherous royal favourite the notorious George 'Bubb' Doddington, who was ultimately raised to the peerage as Baron Melcombe, and who died in 1762. Wings of the house were demolished in 1795, leaving the building a shadow of its former splendour. Bubb, an expert in political chicanery, employed a steward named Doggett who was as crooked as his master. Called upon to give an account of his financial mismanagement, this dishonest steward went into the library and shot himself. It was said that if one lingered by the park gates at midnight, one would see an 18th century bewigged figure, with knee breech-

The nave of Wimborne Minster.

es tied with yellow silk ribbon, awaiting the arrival of his coach. When this eventually drove up, complete with headless horses and coachman, the figure would get into the coach and drive to Eastbury House, where he would go into the library and repeat the whole macabre performance of his suicide.

Of particular interest was the yellow silk ribbon, because Doggett's body was exhumed when the parish church of Tarrant Gunville was pulled down.

To the amazement of the workmen, it was said that the corpse showed no sign of decomposition and the legs were still tied together – with yellow silk ribbon.

Many stories of a ghostly nature associated with Dorset are almost certainly legendary, although some of these legends may be murmurs from the dawn of the county's history, or perhaps long-lost folk memories of past events, forgotten except in the distorted versions handed down orally from generation to generation.

Some such stories, however, are said to have occurred in more recent times. About a century ago, the 16th century structure of Lulworth Castle, built from the stones of nearby Bindon Abbey – could this act of sacrilege have resulted in a curse being placed upon the building? – came into prominence because of the 'Ghostly Glare', a phosphorescent light seen after dark on the walls of one of the bedrooms. Some 19th century psychical researchers maintained that the light was caused by a luminous fungus and suggested that the affected wall be demolished and rebuilt. This was done but the glare remained. Any further chance of solving this 'psychic' mystery was soon lost forever, because in the 1930s the castle was engulfed in flames and has remained a shell ever since.

Some years ago when I was collecting material for a book on Dorset ghosts, I placed a letter in a local newspaper and several of its readers were kind enough to write and tell me of their experiences. One, a Mr Dench then living in Weymouth, told me that in 1934, his father purchased an old farmhouse just outside Weymouth, but then in a very isolated position, the nearest building being a public-house half a mile away. The farmhouse was at that time known as the Iron Box, but as the district has now become a built-up area, it has now been relegated to a fish and chip shop and a mini-market.

As a ten year old boy Mr Dench had just gone to bed one day. It was winter and the room was fairly dark because there were no lights in it, neither were there any in the street outside. He had been in bed for a while when he alleged that from the bedroom door he saw an odd geometric form pass across the room and disappear through the opposite wall. The shape appeared to be quite dense. As there was no light of any sort, it could not have been a shadow. The writer then went to sleep and never mentioned his strange experience until years later in conversation with his mother.

He raised the subject of hauntings in the house, and drew a picture, as well as he could remember of the form. His mother went quite pale and he was amazed when she produced another drawing made by his brother, and absolutely identical. On another occasion my informant was asleep in the room, which was then illuminated by the dancing flames of a roaring fire. No shadows were visible but he distinctly felt his coverlet being forcibly pulled back and at the same time he was conscious of a sharp tap on his upper arm.

An impression of the geometric shape seen at Iron Box farmhouse.

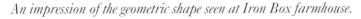

Another time his nine year old sister was asleep in the same bedroom, when she awoke screaming because she felt that she was being forcibly pulled from her bed. Her mother, startled by her screams, hurriedly entered the room to go to her daughter's rescue, and felt she was taking part in a violent tug-of-war with an invisible but menacing force, in her effort to pull her child back into her bed.

When the small branch railway line that used to run from the village of Maiden Newton to the town of Bridport fell a victim to the ruthless Beeching some years ago, some of the former station buildings on the line were converted into attractive residences. An occupant of such a house, sited on the foundations of former Powerstock Station told me that on many occasions, both she and other members of her family, all non-smokers, had been conscious of the aroma of pipe tobacco in different parts of the house, particularly in the area that had once been the passengers' waiting room. At other times they had heard the chugging of little tank engines, similar to those that had used the line in bygone days, and they had heard them thundering over sleepers that had long vanished, and were now completely wrapped in a covering of grass.

Powerstock station.

These then are just a few examples of the stories of personal experiences that have taken place, well into the present century. One often wonders how many other of these ancient and historic sites might have strange stories to tell, if only they could speak, or how many other inhabitants of Dorset are unwilling to tell their stories for fear of ridicule.

We have now traversed the length and breadth of the County of Dorset, and have been told about many of its curiosities. These curiosities all form a part of this fascinating county's rich tradition and history, which in turn, play an important role as a microcosm of our national heritage.

Introducing ...

MICHAEL WILLIAMS, *a Cornishman, started full-time publishing in 1975. He and his wife Sonia live in a cottage on the shoulder of a green valley just outside St Teath in North Cornwall.*

In addition to publishing and writing Michael Williams is a keen cricketer and collector of cricket books and autographs. He was the first captain of the Cornish Crusaders Cricket Club and is today President of the Crusaders. He is also a member of Cornwall and Gloucestershire County Cricket Clubs. A member of the RSPCA and the International League for the Protection of Horses, he has worked hard for reform in laws relating to animal welfare. In 1984 he was elected to The Ghost Club.

His latest book is Supernatural Search in Cornwall *and he is currently collaborating with Polly Lloyd of Bristol on* Somerset Mysteries. *Here he adds a postscript to* Strange Dorset Stories.

DORSET POSTSCRIPT

Michael Williams

THE FACE of Dorset, like the face of a man or woman, can be different things: tender yet harsh, kind but alarming. Dorset is susceptible to mood, deep down capable of being overcast by melancholy.

Paul Nash, writing about Dorset, in 1935, said: '*...the past is always evident in that face. And it is not always the farthest past which is most assertive. There are certain places, at certain times, when the record of some drama can start into life as a scar glows with sudden memory.*'

David Foot, in an early page, warned us: '*There have always been tears . . .*' Yet curiously the face of Dorset is not long distorted by such memory and memories: the changing light, the blue sea, the sheer beauty of the landscape and the villages; and herein lies the enigma that is Dorset.

In the days of Queen Victoria, painters generally held the view that every picture should tell a story: something from history or myth perhaps. For the greater part of a hundred calendars that painterly story-telling has been out of fashion. But, thanks to the renaissance of figurative painting in the British Isles, it is coming back.

Our six contributors have resembled that style of painting. They have told their stories – and told them well.

Browsing through library shelves you are soon very conscious of the enormous creativity of Dorset. It has fired imagination in quite extraordinary fashion.

Thomas Hardy naturally emerges as the literary giant. Some say Hardy is Dorset, but he is more than that, more than an outstanding regional writer.

G.K. Chesterton once reflected: '*. . . when literary critics say that the*

Every picture should tell a story …

tales of Thomas Hardy are full of the 'atmosphere' of Dorsetshire or of Wessex, they do some injustice to what is really powerful in his prose. He had in fact a great love of shapes that are not shadows. He can make a picture which is something more than a picture; because it is not flat. It is like a picture full of coloured statues, and has the depth of a stage. There is something symbolic of him in that minor episode in Tess, when the rascal returns as a revivalist, and paints all along the wide fence across the country-side the large and flaming letters of his gospel. Hardy's gospel could hardly be mistaken for good news. But he painted it in much the same large open-air alphabet; generally as picturesque but always as plain. His novels and poems are full of a sort of solid antics that stick to the memory almost apart from the meaning. They might be called the practical jokes of a pessimist. A very typical example is the poem about the prodigal who, returning home, thinks he sees his father the huntsman afar off, conspicuous by his red coat; when his father has long been dead and the red coat is hung on a scarecrow. That, of course, is very characteristic of Hardy in every aspect: the view of life which is something more than tragic irony and approaches sometimes to a sort of torturers' mockery. But though the dark story is very dark, the red coat is still very bright. The actual technical method is at once lively and materialistic; and it is a little misleading to talk of it as atmosphere. The point is rather in that very vividness and objectivity with which the vermilion coat glows across the empty air. In that little tragedy there is a mistake, but nothing so merciful as a mist.'

Dorset has had a surprisingly large amount of crime – much of it of the killing kind.

Felicity Young chose an interesting murder case. One wonders what kind of verdict Charlotte would have received in the current courtroom climate. I float that question on the strength of something published by Bossiney back in 1975 and now long out of print. In his introduction to *Facets of Crime* Ronald Duncan wrote: *People may argue that murder is always murder and that such crimes as rape have never been condoned. But this is not true. In war, a man can be honoured and rewarded for killing on behalf of his country. Is it, we must ask, more or less of a crime to kill somebody who has injured you than to erase a man you've never met merely because he wears a different uniform? Or, who is the greater criminal: the man who strikes down his neighbour whom he suspects of sleeping with his wife or the bomber pilot who releases destruction upon a hundred women and children whom he has never met? Clearly, we see that war itself is a crime and by it and in it all men become criminals. And it seems to me most probable that more enlightened ages will, if we reach them, regard nationality itself as the twentieth century's greatest crime against mankind. For it is in the name of the Fatherland that such nadirs of humanity such at Katzn, Auschwitz, and Buchenwald were committed. Compare those state-engineered obscenities with such excesses committed by Jack the Ripper, and he is made to look comparatively innocent. One is forced to the conclusion that the bigger the state, the worse its crimes. The mob is always brutal and is not less so by becoming the power behind the state.'*

Within that perspective Charlotte Bryant would almost certainly have got a lenient sentence – possibly even the benefit of the doubt.

But the case of Neville Heath would have still carried the severest sentence – and what a field day the press and the media would have had. First, there was the vicious murder of Margery Gardener by Heath and his diamond weave whip in a hotel bedroom. They say Margery liked being bound and lashed, but this time in offering her naked body to Heath and his whip she was being incredibly reckless. 'Find that whip and you've found your man,' Professor Keith Simpson, told the police, pointing to the diamond-pattern lash marks on the girl's body. The police proceeded to do just that. They found the whip in an attache case left in a railway cloakroom by Heath. But between that discovery and Margery's murder, the monster had committed another at Bournemouth. Heath was denying that he had killed Margery Gardener when officers found the mutilated naked body of Doreen Marshall in Branksome Chine.

At the Old Bailey Heath may have looked handsome and debonair, but he was found guilty. Before going to the scaffold Heath asked for a whisky, and when it was brought to him, he said quite calmly: 'I think I'll make it a double.'

From murder to cricket may seem a gigantic leap – though curiously the only murderer I met was a cricketer – but that is another story and another place. Hereabouts I feel inclined to make a personal response.

David Foot, in his splendid scene-setting opening chapter, asked how a Cornishman should be riveted by Gloucestershire cricket.

It is deeper than the fact that I saw my very first county match on the county ground at Bristol. It is more than a fleeting glimpse of the great Walter Hammond – he scored only four runs – but what runs: a majestic boundary through the covers off the front foot.

Of course, it has something to do with the pride that Jack Crapp, the left hand batsman for Gloucestershire and England was a Cornishman. I always look at the Gloucestershire scores first in the morning paper, and it helped to make my day when J.F. Crapp had made a good score. He was born only a few miles down the road from where I am writing this postscript.

It's all to do with the glorious Gloucestershire past. The Graces, W.G. and E.M., Gilbert Jessop, Zaheer Abbas of Pakistan and, of course, today Jack Russell, immaculate prince of wicket-keepers. John Arlott got to the heart when he once said 'I must confess that I always approach the Gloucestershire ground at Bristol with a higher expectation of memorable cricket than I feel at any other ground. The entire history of Gloucestershire cricket is full, for me, of the names of men who played in the epic manner.'

Through my cricket library I imagine that I saw them all: the bold unconventional captaincy of Beverley Lyon, the magnificent guile

Gimblett – a 'buccaneer of a batsman'.

of Charlie Parker's left arm bowling, the cavalier stroke play of Charles Barnett. In the eye of imagination I have seen such men playing, as Mr Arlott rightly says, 'in the epic manner.'

But I must get back to Dorset whose own county club was formed in 1896. I have vivid memories of Dorset cricket in the Minor Counties: the elegant batsmanship of those cricketing schoolmasters M.M. Walford and G.E.S. Woodhouse, the bowling of Ray Dovey – he wore spectacles and bowled off breaks at medium pace – and most vivid of all the batting of Harold Gimblett after his career with Somerset in the First Class game. Gimblett was a buccaneer of a batsman, a fine driver, he was murderous on anything short of a length. One day I had the luck of an hour-long conversation with him in the pavilion. A complex man, he later committed suicide, and I attended his memorial service at St James's Church, Taunton in May 1978 when John Arlott read the lesson and Alan Gibson gave a moving tribute.

The very first Cornwall match I ever saw was against Dorset on the Truro School ground. Dorset were captained by a gentleman called Mr Harrison who had one good hand and the other badly withered; consequently he batted with only one hand. However he bowled slow leg breaks with considerable cunning, tossing the ball high into the air and wide of the off stump, he invited the batsman to all sorts of indiscretion. Later when Dorset came to play Cornwall at Penzance, I worked the scoreboard and, later still, was promoted to the scorebox where I was the Cornish scorer. So Dorset has a rather special place in my cricketing memories.

Within the boundaries and coastline of Dorset is a great diversity of countryside, and it is the underlying rock which governs what we see, and the haphazard succession of limestone, chalk, sand and clay alters and intensifies the unfolding of this varied landscape. The rocky bays and cliff-lined beaches, the large fields and the small pastures – and that desolate unproductive heath: it is incredible to think all these are to be found inside one English county.

As I come towards the end of this Dorset postscript, I find the word *strange* and its relationship with the county somehow defies neat classification.

Of course, there are strange facets scattered all over the place.

Moreton, the resting place of Lawrence of Arabia, lying in a coffin inscribed: 'T.E.L. who should sleep among kings.' Cerne Abbas, the giant man with fingers seven feet long. How many visitors coming through Tarrant Gunville realise it is the cradle of the camera? Thomas Wedgwood died in 1805 at the age of 34, with his discovery still imperfect, but he had already founded photography on the principle of making pictures by the action of light.

And how about that curious coincidence at Thorncombe 800 years ago? Alice, Viscountess of Devon, encountered a group of monks trudging through the village. The monks told her they were seeking Waverley Abbey in Surrey – now their benefactor had died they must starve unless they reached Waverley. They did not know it, but the benefactor they had lost was the brother of this lady in the Dorset countryside, and, as his heiress, she offered the monks new pastures here and the money to build an abbey.

I am intrigued by Barney Camfield's researches into Arthur and his claim that Dorset, or parts of it, is King Arthur Country. There are parts of Cornwall, which have a strong Arthurian atmosphere,

Bossiney photographer Ray Bishop with a very early camera – Dorset was the cradle of the art of photography.

Polly Lloyd, author of Legends of Dorset, says: 'Dorset is a treasure house of stories … Time has occasionally blurred the edges between fact and fantasy …'

'… a great diversity in the Dorset countryside …'

and certainly you feel an Arthurian presence in sections of Somerset. In my experience though there is nothing remotely Arthurian in the whole of Devon; yet oddly enough before learning of Barney's investigations I felt that Arthurian something here in Dorset, and it is all to do with spirit rather than shape.

We can read *Legends of Dorset* by Polly Lloyd and discover the county is a mine of myth and legend. In it Polly thoughtfully observed: '*Every part of Dorset seems to have its own story. Some are based on the geography of the land, like the magnificent sweep of the pebble beach at Chesil . . . Then there are tales of characters who are remembered because they were cruel or brave or beautiful, people like Lillie Langtry, mistress of Edward VII who lived in Bournemouth. Such characters may belong to reality, but, by their lives, they have become legendary personalities, and therefore belong to the Folklore of Dorset . . . Dorset is a treasure house of stories, happy and sad, funny and macabre. Time has occasionally blurred the edges between fact and fantasy . . .*'

At the end of her fascinating journey across legendary Dorset we wonder whether there can be such a thing as pure myth. As someone who has been investigating various facets of the paranormal for more than a quarter of a century, I am still not totally sure why Dorset has such a large 'other population.'

In 1988 I commissioned Peter Underwood, the President of The Ghost Club and Britain's number one ghost hunter, to write *Ghosts of Dorset*. On reading his manuscript, I was immensely impressed by the diversity of Dorset's hauntings – not just ghostly people but a ghostly white donkey, phantom coach and horses which Thomas Hardy used in *Tess of the D'Urbervilles*, a disembodied hand seeking to be reunited with a body buried well over one hundred miles away in London, and the Portman Hunt including one headless hound.

In a way, Dorset poses more questions than it answers. Often in looking for a solution, we find another query – and maybe that is why Dorset remains such a strange and beautiful place.

Queen Guinevere, who shared a forbidden love with Arthur's most courtly knight, Lancelot. '… I have felt that Arthurian something here in Dorset.'

MORE BOSSINEY BOOKS ...

DORSET MYSTERIES
introduced by Jean Stubbs
Bossiney invites six authors to probe mysterious facets of Dorset.
'Dorset adds a final ingredient of its own – mystery' Margery Hull, Dorset Evening Echo

LEGENDS OF DORSET
by Polly Lloyd
The author explores legendary Dorset, visiting places as diverse as the Sacred Circle at Knowlton and Chesil Beach. Dorset is a mine of myth and folklore.
'Weird happenings ... Polly Lloyd delves through tales ranging from moving rocks to murders ...'
Ed Perkins, Southern Evening Echo

GHOSTS OF DORSET
by Peter Underwood
The President of the Ghost Club explores a whole range of Dorset hauntings. A ghostly white donkey, a world-famous screaming skull, phantom coach-and-horses story which Thomas Hardy used in *Tess of the D'Urbervilles* and a prehistoric 'Peeping Tom' are some of the subjects.
Ghost hunter Peter Underwood has been spook stalking in Dorset uncovering a host of eerie brushes with the Supernatural.'
Bournemouth Advertiser

SUPERNATURAL ADVENTURE
by Michael Williams
Contains a great deal of unpublished material relating to the Supernatural.
'Spiritual healing, automatic writing are just a few of the spectrum of subjects ... neat, well-presented ... easy-to-read volume.'
Psychic News

WESTCOUNTRY MYSTERIES
Introduced by Colin Wilson
A team of authors probes mysterious happenings in Somerset, Devon and Cornwall. Drawings and photographs all add to the mysterious content.
'A team of authors has joined forces to re-examine and probe various yarns from the puzzling to the tragic.'

BOSSINEY'S FIRST WILTSHIRE TITLES ...

WILTSHIRE MYSTERIES
Introduced by David Foot

GHOSTS OF WILTSHIRE
By Peter Underwood, President of the Ghost Club

OTHER RECENT TITLES ...

ABOUT EXMOOR
by Polly Lloyd

DEVON CURIOSITIES
by Jane Langton

SAINTS OF THE SOUTH WEST
by James Mildren

UNKNOWN SOMERSET
by Rosemary Clinch and Michael Williams

DAPHNE DU MAURIER COUNTRY
By Martyn Shallcross

KING ARTHUR IN SOMERSET
by Rosemary Clinch and Michael Williams

We shall be pleased to send you our catalogue giving full details of our growing list of titles for Devon, Cornwall, Dorset, Somerset and Wiltshire and forthcoming publications. If you have any difficulty in obtaining our titles, write direct to Bossiney Books, Land's End, St Teath, Bodmin, Cornwall.